Are You KIDing Me?

51 Things People

Don't Tell You About

Being Pregnant

HALEY GREENE

MORGAN JAMES PUBLISHING • NEW YORK

Are You KIDing Me?

ISBN: 978-1-60037-762-4 (Paperback)
Library of Congress Control Number: 2010922578

Published by:
MORGAN JAMES PUBLISHING
1225 Franklin Ave Ste 32
Garden City, NY 11530-1693
Toll Free 800-485-4943
www.MorganJamesPublishing.com

Cover/Interior Design by:
Rachel Lopez
rachel@r2cdesign.com

Cover Photographs by:
LyraLyra Photography

Habitat for Humanity Peninsula Building Partner

In an effort to support local communities, raise awareness and funds, Morgan James Publishing donates one percent of all book sales for the life of each book to Habitat for Humanity. Get involved today, visit **www.HelpHabitatForHumanity.org**.

Dedication

I would like to dedicate this book to my family for taking such good care of me always, not just during my pregnancy. Uncle Pete, Dorothea and Steve thank you for the comic relief. Cynnie, thank you for doing all the things a mother-in-law should never have to do. My parents Bill and Cris Greene, no daughter could ask for anything more than what you have given to me. Mom, thank you for always being my calming person! Last, but not least to my husband, Stephen thank you for putting up with me through all the good and bad. Most of all thank you for our beautiful daughter! I love you all!

Introduction

My Name is Haley Greene. I owned a clothing store in Tucson for five years. I met a wonderful man after a few years in business and we got married. Like many people we made the decision to start trying to get pregnant, we thought it would take forever, it didn't!! After two months of 'trying" I was pregnant. I sailed through the first couple months with no problem. Everything was fantastic, I even secretly starting making fun of my friends who had morning sickness. The first six months were over in the blink of an eye, then the seventh month came and WHAM everything went downhill, quickly. It seemed everything that could go wrong did. I was on bed rest from the beginning of my seventh month until the day I had my daughter. YUCK! Those three months seemed like an eternity. I had no idea what was going on with my body. I was always asking myself or someone else, <u>Are You Kidding Me</u>??? I didn't know this could happen when you got pregnant! My body could take no more and on December 4th our beautiful daughter was born. In that moment I knew it was all worth it. I decided to take my not very fabulous experience and try to put a funny spin on it in this book. However, I ask myself all the time, who does this more than once???

51 Things People Don't Tell You About Being Pregnant

1.

First things first,
did you know you had to have sex
to get pregnant? And not just once –
In many cases over
and over
and over etc

° ° °

2.

Pupps? What?
        Yes pupps.
No, not nearly as cute as multiple
puppies. It is a horrible pregnancy rash
that you can get. Imagine the worst bug
bite you ever got and multiply it by,
hmm, about A MILLION. It's red and hot
and itchy. Obviously I got it.

Yuck!!!

3.

Do you know you wet your pants
when you sneeze?

Are you <u>kidding</u> me?

4.

You will never be SO HOT in all your life. My husband had to wear fleece from head to toe in the middle of July, because I had to have icicles coming from the air conditioning.

5.

You know those really cute,
very expensive maternity clothes
you can't wait to buy. They won't fit
after your third month.
Unlike the models that are wearing them,
who aren't even pregnant;
you will gain weight EVERYWHERE!!

6.

You can't color your hair?

WAIT a minute!

I don't even know what color my roots are.
Now you want every one else to see them?

Wrong!

HOWEVER, it is an excuse to have weekly manicures. I suppose that's something.

7.

No more acrylic nails ladies.

8.

If you have never had acid reflux before, you are in for a treat.
It single handedly RUINED an entire vacation for myself and everyone around me. Luckily, they are family, so I don't feel too bad. I was the one with the reflux after all.

9.

You will never,
I mean NEVER, sleep through
the night again.
With the peeing
and the hot flashes,
FORGET IT.

Lifetime television was my best friend at 2 am.

that's a Twinkie,
i swear...
they look better at 3a.m.

10.

While you are up in the middle of the
night peeing, you get a little hungry.
I call this sleep eating, since I didnt
remember the next morning eating an
entire box, yes a box, of Twinkies.
Needless to say, I gained a little more
than you are suppose to.

11.

Why isn't my baby 60 lbs?
That's how much I gained!

12.

If you are modest and don't like to have anyone see you naked, pregnancy is not for you. EVERYONE sees you naked. You might as well walk into the Drs' office naked.

It would take less time.

13.

You will be able to see your feet.

HOWEVER,

you will NOT be able to see
your Va-jay-jay!

14.

I know I have bones in my feet.
Why can't I see them?

15.

That is what everyone will say when they see your first ultrasound pictures.

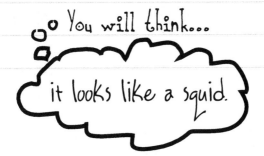

16.

Did you know that babies could have
hiccups while inside of you?
Of course you didn't.

It ~~fells~~ feels, and even worse it looks
like a soccer match is going on
in your stomach. It usually happens
right when you are about to fall asleep.

Thanks!

Anyone's cooking is better than hospital food!

17.

Did you know that bed rest meant stay in bed?
I thought it meant don't leave the property.

Be very careful with this.

If you don't follow directions your doctor may put you in the hospital to make sure you stay in bed.

I am a slow learner.

I am a slow learner.

I am a slow learner.

I am a slow learner.

I am a slow learner.

I am a slow learner.

I am a slow learner.

I am a slow learner.

I am a slow learner.

I am a slow learner.

I am a slow learner.

I am a slow learner.

I am a slow learner.

I am a slow learner.

I am a slow learner.

I am a slow learner.

I am a slow learner.

I am a slow learner.

I am a slow learner.

18.

If you call the Drs office at 5:01 p.m.
with a question or problem,
you WILL be spending the rest
of your evening at the hospital.

It took me 5 times to figure it out.

19.

Okay, you can't drink and you can't smoke.
I get that.

But no morning coffee?

That's where I draw the line!!

zzzzzzzz

20.

Everything is VERY dramatic.
You get a cold,
YOU COULD DIE!

You get diarrhea,
YOU COULD DIE!

(You won't, but you'll wish you had!)

21.

DO NOT go online to self diagnose yourself

YOU COULD DIE!

SHOPPING LIST

carrots

bananas

vitamins

shampoo

cupcakes ✓

juice

lettuce

bread

22.

Do not, I repeat, do not go to the grocery store hungry.

You <u>will</u> only come home with things covered in frosting.

23.

Buy a really cute, really comfortable pair of slippers. They will be the ONLY shoes that fit your feet when you leave the hospital.

Leave the Manolo's at home.

24.

Actually, put your very expensive high heels in a box. You will only be able to look at them now.
Because what no one told you,

YOUR FEET GROW! Are you kidding me?

Helen?

    hadley?

Hannah?

    harry?

      Halee?

25.

You WILL forget your own name.

Don't even bother trying to remember anyone elses.

26.

DO NOT give anyone your house key
unless you are ok with waking up
from a nap to people standing over you.

Very creepy!!

~~brenda~~

~~debbie~~

~~allison~~

cynthia

~~sabrina~~

~~anna~~

top Secret

~~jerry~~

~~michael~~

justin

~~rick~~

~~andrew~~

~~sean~~

Top secRet

27.

Do not tell ANYONE what names
you have in mind for the baby
unless, you want people telling you
they have a cousin,

⬇︎

who has a friend,

⬇︎

who is a stripper in New Jersey
with the same name!

28

You will trip over EVERYTHING
and nothing.

Air will somehow manage to get in your way.

For those of you less fortunate, you WILL have to do this a 2nd time. But this time they take your blood every hr for 3 VERY long, VERY hungry hrs. By the time it is over you are ready to chew your own arm off!

Guess how long I had to sit there!!

29.

You will have to have a gestational diabetes test. You can't eat for 12 hrs. Once you get to the lab for the test you have to drink a very thick liquid version of orange crush. So now you are hungry and all cracked out on sugar and all you can do is sit in the waiting room for an hr until they can draw your blood.

30.

People will ask you all through
your pregnancy how much weight
you have gained?
Likes it's a competition.
Do what you will, but my advice. LIE!!!

No matter what you say, EVERYONE has an opinion!

31.

All the women you know that
"LOVE" being pregnant ... they are LYING!!
Or on really good meds.
If that's the case, get some for yourself.

top Secret

Shhh, don't tell anyone.

Bring your own over-the-counter meds to the hospital.

Otherwise ONE Maalox will cost you $100.00? You know insurance is NOT going to pick that up!!

33.

Once you are pregnant you don't really matter anymore. Your family only cares about their new grandbaby and the Drs are keeping you healthy because you are now just the "housing unit."

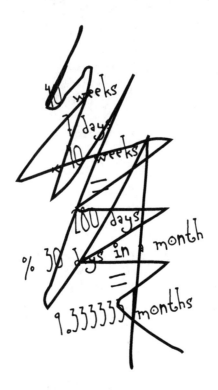

40 weeks

7 days

40 weeks

=

280 days

% 30 days in a month

=

9.333333 months

40 weeks

% 4 weeks in a month

=

not 9 months!!!

34.

9 months.
That's how long everyone says
you are pregnant.
Until you meet with your Dr. All of
a sudden you are pregnant for 40 weeks.
I don't know what kind of math anyone
else does, but 40 weeks
DOES NOT equal 9 months.

35

Do not have a birthing plan in mind, because your baby did not get that memo! It is his or her show. Remember you are JUST the "housing unit."

36.

Despite what your significant other has heard
you DON'T turn into Jenna Jameson
and want sex all day and night.
However, if you are one of the few that aren't
too tired to give sex a try... be careful.
If your nipples are stimulated you could go into
labor. I bet he's not GETTING ANY anymore.

Sorry guys.

37.

You may have heard that breastfeeding hurts.
The only reason it hurts is because your
breasts, that use to be the size of a walnut,
have now swollen to the size
of a cantaloupe.
The baby has nothing to do with it.

Those suckers just hurt!!!

38.

I never knew why nursing pads came in bulk. If you don't have a Costco or Sams Club card, you better go get one. You are going to need lots of those pads.

Imagine Lake Michigan in your bra and trying to soak it up. SEXY!

You are JUST the
"housing unit!!"
Did I mention that?

39.

If you are a back sleeper, be prepared to change your ways. You must now sleep on your side.

Ah ah, not just any side, your left side only, please!! **Why you ask??** To get proper air to the baby this is the best position.

40.

1. Everyone wants to feel the baby move inside of you. Yes, I mean everyone. The creepy old guy in the grocery store? Yep, he's coming over to lay his sticky, dirty fingers on your stomach!

41.

You WILL look 11 months pregnant
when you leave the hospital.
Some moron will ask when you are due.
Take a deep breath and walk away
or tackle them ... your choice.

42.

You're meeting at 10:00? 10:00 p.m.?
That's 2 hrs past my bedtime.

Say goodbye to your friends without babies.
You will never see them again.

They still have a social life.

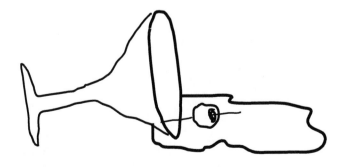

43.

I'm sure you have heard that cocoa butter
prevents stretch marks.

It worked for me, but I almost lost
an arm in the process. I would wake up
in the middle of the night smelling
like a giant chocolate bar.

I didn't know who
was going to take the first bite.
My husband or me!

♥ Thanks Granny O.

44.

If you don't get along with your
mother-in-law, now is the time
to make sure she is your best friend.
She may be the only one you can count on
to hold your hand while the nursing student
is TRYING to put a catheter in you.

TO THE MEN, no woman is <u>ever</u> going to feel bad for you if you think you are having morning sickness. So get up, tell your woman how beautiful she is and go buy her a tub of ice cream!!

45.

If your significant other is anything like my husband he will get every pregnancy symptom known to "man." So go ahead, give him that evil stare you have been thinking about, then hand him this book and tell him now read this...

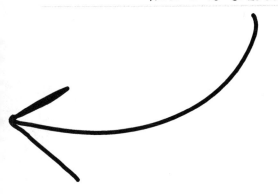

46.

Because you have gained weight EVERYWHERE, go buy the most comfortable sweatpants and tee shirts you can find. It Will be your new uniform!

Watch how a cow is milked.
That's what someone
will be doing to you at 3 a.m.

NICE!!

47.

Breast feeding. Easy right?
Just put the baby up there and go!
WRONG!!

You have to teach the baby
how to nurse and all the nurses
have to teach you.

48

Oh My God, some men think pregnant women are hot. Yes, random men will whistle at you while you are trying to buy a box of candy bars at your local convenience store. SUPER!

49.

If you are like me you have tried for 21 plus years to avoid getting pregnant, so you are in utter shock when the pregnancy test is positive.

If you call your mom first, panicking, don't tell your husband. Mine still won't let me forget that he was the second person to know I was pregnant.

OOPS!

WE
ARE NOT HAVING A BABY!!!

50.

I don't know about you, but I was ready to strangle my husband if he said one more time "WE'RE HAVING A BABY!" When was the last time you heard of a man pushing something

the size of a pot roast

through a hole the

size of a lemon

and living

to tell about it?

51.

People volunteer to do this again?

ARE YOU NUTS???!!!

She was DEFINITELY worth it!

Printed in the USA
CPSIA information can be obtained
at www.ICGtesting.com
JSHW012042140824
68134JS00033B/3204